SCHIRMER'S LIBRARY
OF MUSICAL CLASSICS

Vol. 849

O. ŠEVČIK

Op. 9

Preparatory Exercises in Double-Stopping

In Thirds, Sixths, Octaves and Tenths

For the Violin

Edited by

PHILIPP MITTELL

ISBN 978-0-7935-4800-2

G. SCHIRMER, Inc.

DISTRIBUTED BY

7777 W. BLUEMOUND RD. P.O. BOX 13819 MILWAUKEE, WI 53213

EXERCISES IN DOUBLE-STOPPING

Doppelgriff-Übungen

Man übe jedes Beispiel und jede Variante in folgenden Tonarten, gestossen und gebunden:

Exercises in Double-stopping.

Practise each exercise and each variante in the following keys, both détaché and legato:

① In Des und Ges wird der erste und letzte Takt der Beispiele nicht gespielt.

① In Db and Gb major the first and last measures of the exercises are omitted.

*) Siehe Anmerkung zu Op. 8.
*) See Note to Op. 8.

17671

3.

Sexten.

Sixths.

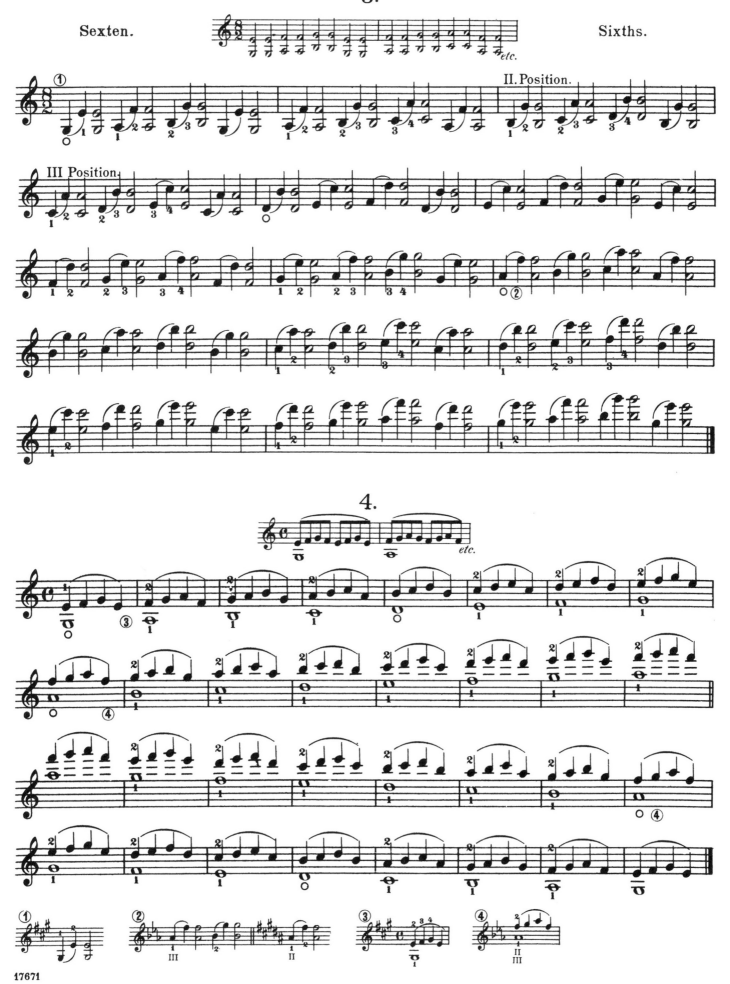

4.

4

5.

Terzen.   Thirds.

6.

7.

Quarten.   Fourths.

17671

11.

Sexten.   Sixths.

12.

13.

14.

Terzen. Thirds.

15.

16.

Secunden. Seconds.

Quarten.   **17.**   Fourths.

18.

Oktaven.   **19.**   Octaves.

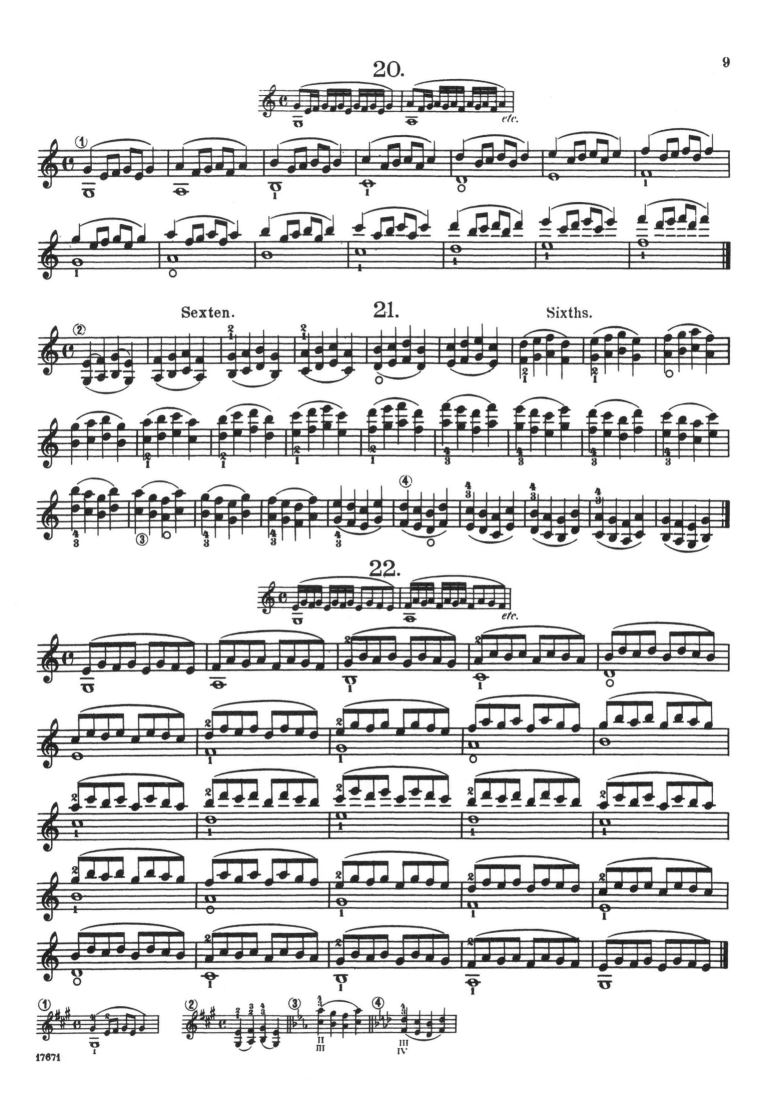

Terzen.

Thirds.

Oktaven.

29.

Octaves.

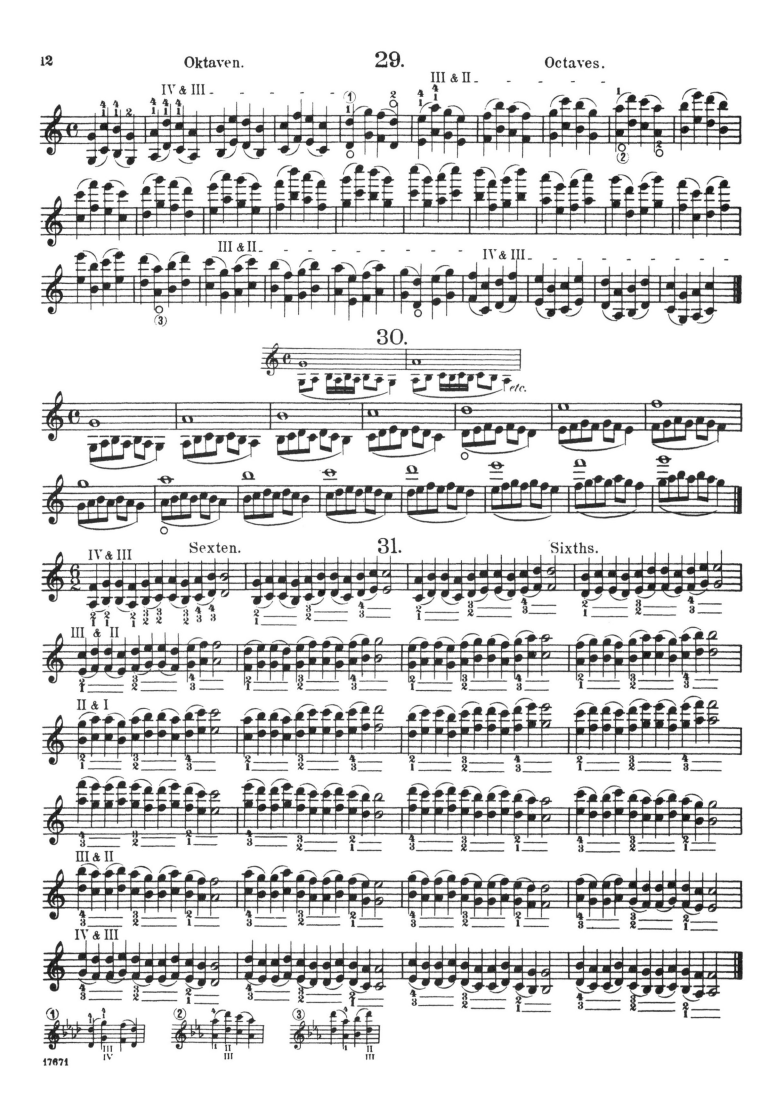

13

35.

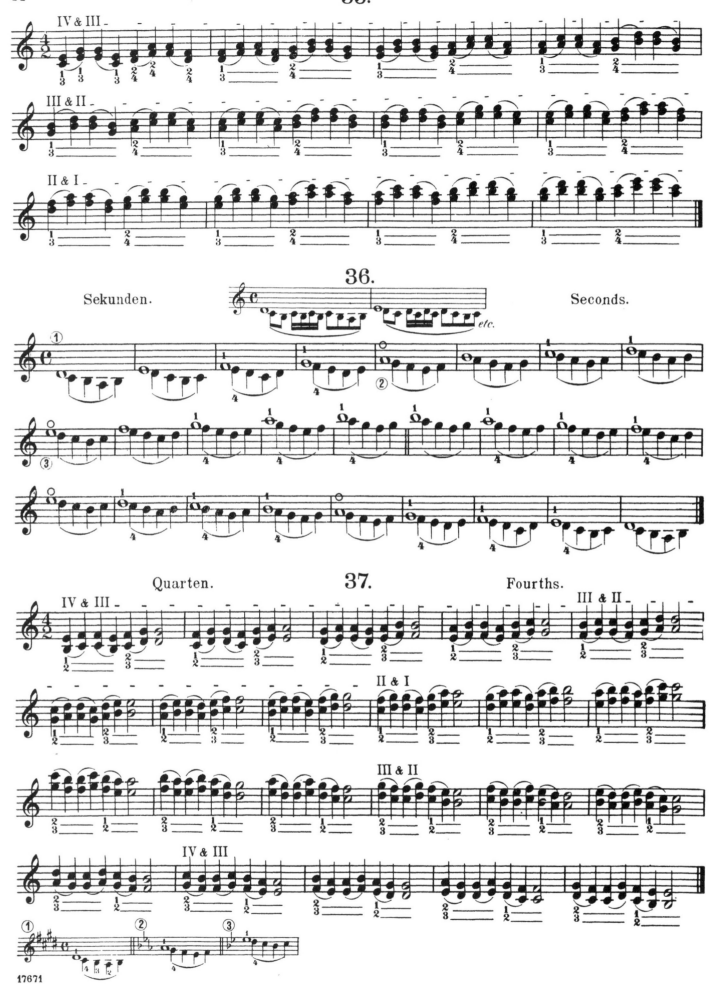

Sekunden.   # 36.   Seconds.

Quarten.   # 37.   Fourths.

38.

39.

Dezimen.
Tenths.

40.

Oktaven.
Octaves.

47.

48.

Dezimen.
Tenths.

IV & III

III & II

III & II

IV & III

49.

Sexten.
Sixths.

Oktaven. 50. Octaves.

Quarten. 51. Fourths.

Sexten. 52. Sixths.

17671

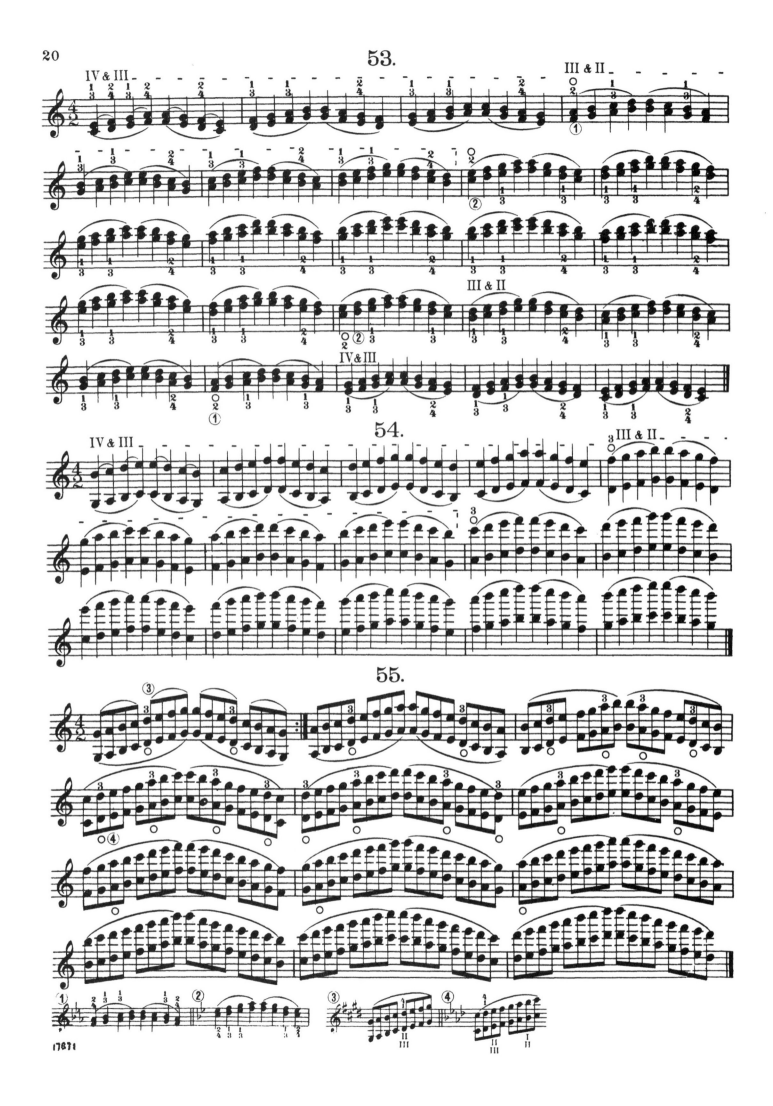

MELODIOUS DOUBLE-STOPS

(Mélodies en Doubles-Cordes)

FOR VIOLIN

by

JOSEPHINE TROTT

BOOK I

G. SCHIRMER, Inc.

DISTRIBUTED BY
HAL•LEONARD®